GW00658412

# MORE Cats
## OF THE
## GREEK ISLANDS

HANS SILVESTER

THAMES AND HUDSON

Translated from the French
LES CHATS DU BONHEUR
by Jane Brenton

The photographs in this book were
taken with Leica M6 and R6 cameras,
using Kodachrome 64 and 100 film

This edition copyright © 1996 Thames and Hudson Ltd, London
Copyright © 1995 Editions de La Martinière, Paris

All rights reserved. No part of this book may be reproduced or
transmitted in any form or by any means, electronic or mechanical,
including photocopy, recording or any other information storage and
retrieval system, without prior permission in writing from the publisher

British Library Cataloguing-in-Publication Data

A catalogue record for this book is available from the British Library

ISBN 0-500-01694-1

Printed and bound in France

There are quite a few things that a cat requires to live happily: food and drink, obviously, as well as shelter, a quiet place to sleep and a patch of dirt to perform his natural functions; but more than all of these, he needs a human being who loves him.

And yet those are just the basic requirements. To be truly happy, he will need much more than that – a territory of his own, where he can satisfy his hunting instinct, a spot where he can meet other cats in the neighbourhood, a companion to play with, a tree for climbing and sharpening his claws, a widely varied diet. These are things many cats have to do without, but the biggest lack of all for today's cats is a communal life, contact with other cats.

Judging by my observations in Greece, cats that run free choose to live as a tribe. The group permits the individual to be with the others or on his own, depending on how he feels at the time – just like people, in fact. The group is always headed by an elderly she-cat or queen, the clan's leader, who is full of experience and always ready to defend any of them against attacks from outside. It is she who knows the territory best; it is almost always she who brings back living prey to teach the young ones how to hunt. Frequently she and her daughters suckle and rear their young in common. Several males can co-exist within the group without problems, but there appears always to be one dominant male who is highly respected by the rest. This cat has an excellent relationship with the dominant elderly queen, often his own mother. The two of them stand out because they have a different air about them and because of their very strong personalities. Anywhere in the world, these are always the cats who are favoured by the people looking after them: we should not forget that on the Greek islands cats do not have any one owner, they roam free out of doors.

I try to show in my photographs just how rich and intense a life cats lead within their family or society, and how much happiness they derive from life within the group.

When we have a cat in our home, we actually know very little about him. To get to know a cat properly, we need the opportunity to see him in contact with others of his kind.

In the restricted area of a small village, male and female cats know one another extremely well; they can recognize one another from a distance and can choose to avoid or seek out paticular encounters, thus simplifying relationships considerably. As a form of friendly greeting, they rub noses, their tails curling around the other's body. Both toms and queens defend their territories, this being the sole cause of the terrible fights

that often end in serious injury. These appalling territorial battles take place in silence; the howling you hear at night is usually made by a queen in heat defending herself against unwelcome male approaches. The male cat undergoes a transformation in moving from birth to adulthood, the adorable little kitten gradually turning into a great big bristling tomcat.

Our own cats have always been – and still are – very discreet as regards their amorous activities; these take place at night, in secret places. Even if one lives in the country, where a cat is free to come and go at will, one only ever sees him on his own as he jealously preserves the mystery surrounding his encounters.

To help you understand why I have devoted so many years of patient attention to these observations of cats in Greece, I would like to introduce you to the cats who have lived with us in Provence. It was they who gave me a better understanding of the complex nature of cats, and made me take more than a passing interest in

their behaviour. For thirty-five years now, they have shared our house, enriched our lives and brought us happiness.

Deprived of cats, a house in the country is a sad house, lacking an essential element. It is also prey to rats and mice. Peasants understand that; there is at least one cat on every farm.

You quickly become accustomed to having a cat. In a very short time, he takes his place in the life of his human companions, for you do not own a cat, rather you share your life with him. In the most natural way imaginable, he becomes co-owner of the house and its surroundings. In his own way, he feels himself to be a member of the family, on an equal footing with the rest.

In 1961, a friend gave us our first black-and-white cat, Peter, who was with us for more than ten years. I often think of him returning to the house seriously wounded after terrible fights, demanding to be looked after, in order to set off again as quickly as possible on the next round of adventures.

Our house forms part of a small hamlet on a hillside, at the edge of cultivated fields; beyond that is scrubland. It is a place that offers a good life for people and cats alike. The house is very old, over three hundred years, and has been occupied by many generations of people and an incalculable number of cats. Cats love old houses and all that goes with them. They love the old trees growing nearby; in our house they love the inner courtyard with its old fig tree and vine. The numbers living in our hamlet have declined, and where there were formerly sixteen households there are now only four families left, each with cats. Most of the domestic animals – sheep, goats, donkeys, horses and rabbits – that used to live in the hamlet have disappeared; now only two dogs, some cats, hens and pigeons survive. The cat is unique among domestic animals, being both more independent and more attached to his home.

Another very significant peculiarity of cats is that they have never been put to work for us, no one has ever succeeded in training them; equally, they have never provided us with anything, and we don't kill and eat them. True, they are very useful for hunting down the rats and mice that used to spread terrible epidemics. But the main reason why cats are to be found throughout the world is to do with their charm and grace, the sheer physical pleasure of stroking them.

Francisco was Peter's successor, and she lived with us for eighteen years. She was given to us as a male, with a male name, and we thought that was what she was until her well-rounded belly provided evidence to the contrary! She had three litters of kittens, which we reared and then gave away to neighbours. Francisco was living with us when our daughter was born, and she always demonstrated a complete understanding of the situation, quite happy to let herself be used as a toy, with never the slightest problem. A child learns a lot from being with a cat, above all that there are limits you must not go beyond, for if you do the cat will defend itself or simply walk away. In our family, a true friendship grew up between girl and animal. This tabby cat of ours was a remarkable hunter; in the course of her life she must have brought literally hundreds and hundreds of mice into the courtyard to eat. But curiously, she showed no interest whatsoever in any mice inside the house. For her, they were no longer prey. We were forced to catch them with traps, even though it was she who had let them escape indoors. She was very independent and we were the only ones allowed to stroke her. For a cat living in the country, eighteen years is a very long life indeed, and Francisco died quietly and peacefully of old age. We buried her at the end of the vegetable garden.

Later we had a cat called Greco with fine reddish-brown stripes, who seemed to draw himself up tall on his paws. He shared his life with us for a year, but after that became increasingly inquisitive and independent; his territory extended further and further from the house. We used to worry about him, especially when we returned home late at night and saw foxes in our headlights. Unfortunately, in Provence there are things much more dangerous than foxes, namely hunters, not only because of the poison they put down for the foxes, which accounts for many a cat and dog, but also because there is not much game about and some hunters practise taking pot shots at cats in the country, even quite close to farms and hamlets.

If he wants to, our cat can stay in the house all day but, following the custom of Provençal peasants, we always put him out at night to catch mice. In the morning he waits to be let back in and likes to join us for breakfast. To our great regret, he cannot tell us the story of his night-time exploits, but it is quite clear that he has had very little sleep and is much more tired in the morning than in the evening. We can only imagine his adventures. After his return, he cleans himself thoroughly, licking away the traces of the night's experiences before lapsing into a state of total relaxation, and then sleep. It is truly a double life he leads, spending his days with human beings and at night leading the life of a wild cat. If he is not there in the morning, the house feels sadly empty.

One fine day, Greco simply disappeared. We searched for him in the village and in the surrounding countryside, but with no luck, not a trace. We missed him terribly; he left a great emptiness. Greco was no ordinary cat, he had become a true friend. I had found him in Greece as a tiny kitten, half-dead with hunger.

Once again, we were conscious of a gap in our lives and decided to go to the SPA, the Society for the Protection of Animals, hoping to find a kitten. First we were shown adult cats shut up in a cage, a sorry spectacle with their troubled gaze and dull fur. Then we saw two kittens in an aviary. When they saw us they began to climb up the wire like monkeys, showing us their pretty little tummies. One of the kittens was black and white, the other a tabby. We immediately decided on the tabby, a small female, and an hour later she was exploring our inner courtyard. We called her Hydra, after the Greek island where Greco came from.

Hydra had a particular talent for climbing and quickly found spots where she could be completely secure, on window sills which she reached via the branches of the fig tree. There she could see without being seen. She had an inborn love of the hunt, which was by far her favourite game. She amused herself by playing with all sorts of insects and was often stung by

wasps and bees. She caught her first mice at a very tender age and was only six months old when she brought home her first rat, almost as big as she was. She was very sweet-natured and had complete trust in us, and in everybody she met. The inner courtyard was her kingdom, and she much preferred it to the house. In the summer, our habit is to spend our days in the courtyard, and she used to love being so close to us and sharing our life to the full.

That year, we travelled to Greece in mid-September, leaving the house in the care of our daughter and her boyfriend. Over the phone, we learned that Hydra had disappeared – once again it was autumn, the hunting season.

We were on yet another of our trips to the island of Hydra, and quickly determined to bring home one of the little kittens that are born in the autumn and stand little chance of surviving through the winter. What happens is that a lot of people leave the island at that time of year, the fishermen have a constant battle with the weather, the cats have less to eat and many of the kittens succumb. In the harbour, we found a grey-and-white kitten under an old abandoned boat. I was certainly the first human being ever to touch him. He was scarcely bigger than my hand but he fought like a little devil. He became our Greco II. At first, back at the hotel, he was wild, and very nervous, but from the third day

he accepted us. He behaved perfectly on the flight from Athens to Marseilles – travelling as a stowaway.

All the cats who have lived with us have had very pronounced characters, very distinct personalities. They have all been highly independent and at the same time very affectionate. We have noticed that there is as much difference between male and female cats as between men and women.

Greco II is the first cat I could legitimately accuse of being an egotist. He has succeeded in gaining an entrée into all the village houses, where he is regarded as a welcome visitor, and indeed a neighbour who is not over-keen on cats even refers to him as Monsieur Greco. He has a powerful personality and feels very sure of himself in any situation, giving off an air of calmness and strength. Indoors, he permits himself to be stroked; outside, it is he who decides whether to approach you or not. He grooms himself with great care and is always impeccable. He doesn't bite or scratch, but if something upsets him, he makes it very clear that you had better watch out – his claws and teeth are ready. He takes himself very seriously, has a sense of his own importance, and never fails to show it; he assumes that he will be the one to make the decisions. He really is an egotist. The fact that he is exceptionally beautiful only emphasizes his character; he is pale grey, with white paws, pink nose and green eyes. Indoors, his favourite spot is an armchair in front of the fire.

Every year in winter, the heavens decree a certain number of days best spent indoors by the fire: days of fierce mistral, snowfalls to the north. You fear for the roof tiles, you feel the heating will give up the unequal struggle. Cats sense the arrival of this sort of weather long before it comes. They refuse to leave the house. Greco plays possum on the hearth, hides his eyes under his paws so that he will neither see nor hear the storm. He can spend a whole day like this in front of the fire. He is not really asleep, just waiting for the return of the good weather.

Our daughter is Greco's best friend. When she comes to visit, he goes to her immediately to be stroked. He sucks the cloth of her blouse or jersey, imitating the treading movements of a kitten at its mother's teat. He purrs very loudly, since this is the height of bliss for him. He loves to play. If he sees another cat, he tries to persuade it to join in. He runs over the open ground, climbs the almond tree as fast as he can, then jumps on to a roof; the race continues through the hamlet, and then the two cats tire and start a friendly wrestling match, biting and scratching but not trying to injure one another. Gradually the game becomes fiercer; a few hairs fly; the fighters begin to hurt each other and start to yowl; then suddenly it is all over and each departs without so much as a backward glance at the other.

Greco is no more than a mediocre hunter, but is proud to come up to you with his prey, still alive, in his jaws. You have to congratulate him before he will eat his victim. He leaves nothing; sparrows disappear feathers and all. He does not, in fact, spend all that much time with us – just a few hours a day. His natural authority is fully respected by the other cats in the hamlet. Even with strange cats he imposes his presence, always ready to attack, never backing down. Greco has been living with us for two years now and he still surprises us with the way he behaves. He is without doubt the most interesting cat who has shared our four walls; he is an important part of our life.

For a short while now, we have also had a female cat inherited from an elderly neighbour

who was forced for health reasons to return to the United States. It was very hard for her to leave without her beloved Kitty, but there was no question of the cat accompanying her into an old people's home. The lady hesitated to mention this impending separation to us, so, leaving enough food in her garden to last for a few days, she departed. Feeling guilty about it, she didn't dare ask us to look after her cat. Kitty,

however, had sensed long before the woman's departure that her life was about to change. She knew that even before hunger prompted her, and came to us immediately. All cats have this gift of sensing changes before they happen. Within a few hours Kitty had grasped that we were her future. She is a tabby with black stripes on her sides. Greco is not all that fond of her. He tolerates her, taking care to show who is boss.

*I know an island in the Cyclades where there are more cats than people. The inhabitants are either fishermen or peasants. Two little grocery shops, a* kafeneion *that is open all the year round, a few rooms to rent from the residents, no hotel. The ferry arrives twice a week and only in calm weather. As well not to mention its name: the island way of life hangs in a precarious balance and I would not want tourists to flock there. The paths were trodden out by donkeys, there are no roads, and therefore no cars either, although the houses do have running water, electricity and television. Everyone knows everyone. The men like to chat in the café, and you are more likely to find the priest with them there than in his church. Life on the island has always been difficult and still is today. If you are prepared to work hard, the land and sea can provide enough to live simply, but it is almost impossible to earn money. The young people have been, and still are, forced to leave the island to work on the boats or in Athens, or even to emigrate to the United States, if they are going to earn at least enough to get married and build a house. The young men, therefore, have travelled, have known a different life, have learned English and, above all, have learned to appreciate the advantages and disadvantages of life on their little island. Those who return have made the positive decision to live there, sharing their life with the cats – and these abound in such numbers that you simply cannot live on this island unless you do like them. If you look out to sea, you see cats on board the boats; if you go to the café, you are surrounded by them; you find them in the streets, outside the houses. The centre of their life is the harbour, which is the source of their food, fish. The catch is consumed on the spot by both the inhabitants and their cats, who benefit from the fishermen's extraordinary generosity. It is only in winter when the weather is bad that the cats go hungry. Then it is that the forces of nature intervene to maintain an equilibrium: the weakest animals die. Mathematically, the growth of a cat population is such that either nature or man has to keep their numbers constant. I have often returned to this island and each time I have observed the same happy harmony existing between the inhabitants, visitors and cats. It is a small world, and it is easy for an observer to place himself right at the heart of these interconnected lives. All you have to do is watch: the village is transformed into a sort of theatre, the cats of course being the star performers. Patience and discretion are all you need to witness their behaviour. Their private life is conducted in the street; you merely have to observe them over a period without disturbing them. I think our cats at home are happy cats. Those I have photographed in Greece are not as spoiled and have a harder life, but they live together in families and as part of a tribe; their relationship with man is of a wholly different kind, and their happiness a different sort of happiness.*

*I spent a lot of time observing the cats of the Greek islands and came to know them well – they recognized me from a distance every time I went back – but of course my relationship with our cats at home in Provence is of a different order altogether.*

*Hans Silvester*